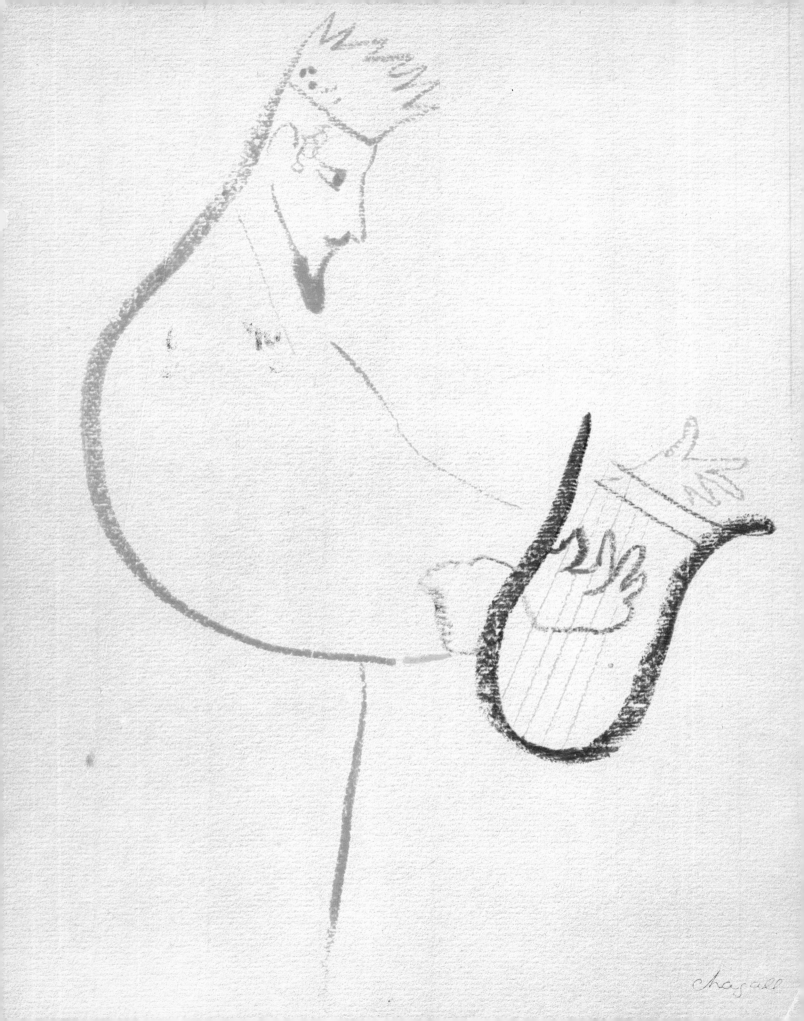

ISRAEL

Preface by

ANDRE MALRAUX

Photographs by

IZIS

Cover and frontispiece by

CHAGALL

Edited by

Nicolas Lazar and Izis

THE ORION PRESS—NEW YORK

Distributed by Crown Publishers Inc.

ACKNOWLEDGMENTS

The Preface and other material from the French have been translated by John Buchanan-Brown.

The poem on Page 18 has been translated by Zahava Albert and is reprinted by her permission.

"With every rolling stone," on Page 42; "Jerusalem is begirt with mountains," on Page 110; and "The Kid from the Haggadah," on Page 138, have been translated by Sholom J. Kahn. The first two are from *Israel Argosy*, published by the Youth and Hechalutz Department of the World Zionist Organization, Jerusalem, Israel. Reprinted by permission of Sholom J. Kahn.

"Beautiful Height! O joy! the whole world's gladness!" on Page 42, is from *Selected Poems of Jehudah Halevi*, translated by Nina Salaman, published by the Jewish Publication Society of America, 1925.

The quotations on Page 54 are from: *Anne Frank: The Diary of a Young Girl*. Copyright 1952 by Otto H. Frank. Copyright 1952 by The American Jewish Committee, reprinted by permission of Doubleday & Co. Inc.

The translation of "I behold graves of ancient time," on Page 92, is from *Selected Poems of Moses Ibn Ezra*, translated by Solomon Solis-Cohen, published by the Jewish Publication Society of America, 1934.

The translation on Page 106 originally appeared in *Flag of Freedom*, published by the Jewish National Fund, Jerusalem, Israel. Permission to reprint has been granted by the translator, Misha Louvish.

The quotation on Page 134 is from *Thieves in the Night* by Arthur Koestler. Copyright 1946 by Arthur Koestler, reprinted by permission of The Macmillan Company.

Other translations in this volume are by Naomi Rosenberg Sarlin, Gloria Goldreich and Renée Koltun.

For Jenka Sperber

This book opens with the words of Chateaubriand and the desert of the Old Testament, the desert which "has never dared break the silence that followed the voice of the Almighty." It closes with the words of the prophet Isaiah, "Watchman, what of the night?—The morning cometh, and also the night" and with the rifle of the Israeli sentry who seems to hold the frontier against the Arabs, the dusk and the Almighty himself.

"Photographic books" were born as eyewitness accounts, travellers' trophies and travelogues, but they soon escaped the tourist's snapshot album and captured the purposeful mood of the documentary films devoted to Dnieperstroi or Tennessee, to the struggle of man against the elements. But the best contemporary books of this class owe their individuality and their art to their exchange of a more complex and mysterious mood for the direct message of the didactic period. Their photographs gain impact less from what they state individually than from what they suggest in mass. (The technique which appeared to exist solely to catch the fleeting instant becomes an art when it seizes the instant that mirrors centuries of history, the instant that alters reality, in holding it up to poetic scrutiny.)

A difficult art and one which has certain advantages is applied to a people who, though often to all appearance annihilated, still gaze out through the oldest eyes in the world. Izis, once again, has not attempted to exalt the building-site and the tractor in his photographs; instead he has shown that Israeli history is something more than the collective farm or hydroelectric scheme. Into our modern age he has loosed the majestic storms of a spiritual obsession. If the girl who laughs across the desert is something more than a goat girl who has escaped the ghetto, it is because she is in correspondence with the splashes of white sheep and black horse on the burning rocks of Carmel. It is easy for a photographer to give expression to happiness for he has only to catch a moment's laughter: perhaps he must be singularly skilled or rarely fortunate for his pictures to match the child so happily answering the teacher's description of the Wailing Wall with, "Now they'll only need three walls to build the Temple." The finest photograph in the book challenges the new building at Misketh-Askelon, the streets of Tel Aviv, or the mounted sentry; a chaldean arch carries three posters, one official, one political and one for a cinema showing a double bill of blood and dreams, an American film on *Mein Kampf* and *The Thief of Bagdad;* below, on the ground, sits an old beggar, another Job, sleeping the sleep of a prophet. A few pages on, but how many years away, an old man like him watches children planting the Martyrs' Forest, whose six million trees will grow on the hills of Jerusalem as a memorial to Hitler's victims.

The photographs are counter-balanced by admirable textual matter which does not attempt connected narrative, but which gives many of the plates an eloquent gravity, and makes them part of that vestigal timelessness which neither war nor the machine age can root out of Israel. "The sun rose on the face of the earth when Lot entered Zoar," says Genesis of the sands that cover Sodom. Opposite a photograph of young soldiers stands the prophetic poem in which Alterman answers the famous remark: "No State is handed over on a silver platter."

> *Then slowly towards the waiting throng*
> *Two step forth—a girl and a boy*
>
> *Clad for work and for war,*
> *Heavy-shod and still,*
> *Up the winding path they make their way . . .*
>
> *. . . Dumb they approach. Are they living or dead?*
> *Who knows, as they stand unmoving there.*

Then Israel questions them and, at peace, they reply:

> *We are the silver platter, on which*
> *The Jewish State is handed you.*

Not the least among the qualities of this book is the way in which sunlight and even joy has been used to convey the gloom of Endor which enshrouds the two figures (we know not whether they live or whether they were executed), and to have fathomed the undercurrent which now aids, now thwarts, is now unrealised, now apparent, and which sets the anxious Israeli epoch apart from the ventures of the pioneers.

The Western pioneers obeyed one of the most powerful calls of the blood; America continues a European trend. The Israeli are no continuation but rather a metamorphosis of the Israelites. That can be attributed to modernisation; the Israeli is to his grandfather in caftan what the streets of Tel Aviv are to the alleys of a Polish ghetto. But that is to overlook the fact that the grandson is a fighter while the grandfather let himself be killed, that the discovery of courage in the Western sense of the term is much more significant than the imitation's skyscraper, and that the Israeli do not owe their courage to the streets of Tel Aviv, but the streets of Tel Aviv to their courage.

They had but one traditional hero, Judas Maccabaeus, and he was regarded less as a hero of revolt than as one of sacrifice. Israel possessed no cycle of heroic verse, hence it was assumed that courage was alien to her. But lack of courage suggests, in the West, weakness, and the Jews have outlasted all the empires that enslaved them. We are really dealing with a quality no less effective than the courage of the soldier but very different from it. Historians have found that though these communities might lack soldiers they had their martyrs, even if it was hard to pick them out of the piles of victims that hid them.

Israel was perhaps the only Eastern people who took God at his word. Martyrdom was by no means ridiculous because the martyr was God's witness; the courage of the soldier was ridiculous because the final victory was in the hands of God alone. Men were not created to conquer, to convert or to wipe out the infidel, but to unite to praise God together. The same sand that covers the Macedonian lance or the Roman eagle will cover the sword of Islam; God remains—and His teaching.

Akiba, the sage of Israel, joined the rebels under Bar Kokhba, but the Rabbi Yochanan ben Zakkai, neither less sage nor less illustrious, accepted the submission of the Jews to the Romans on condition that the Torah be preserved. The Teaching would ensure, more assuredly than rebellion, the survival of an indestructible people who believed only in their soul's immunity. Thus the school that Yochanan set up at Yawnek preserved the Jerusalem for which Akiba died. The Zionist state was born from courage; *without it* even the financial assistance from the United States would have been in vain; without it Zionism would never have realised its utopian dreams. Martyred nations are nations of victims for longer than they are nations of martyrs. One thread of Jewish history runs from their submission to the Persian law whereunder the price of blood was paid in *black money* (copper money without honour) if the blood was Jewish, right up to the last battles in Warsaw where the Jews fought without hope for an honour born on the Palestinian earth, to Jerusalem besieged and to the lonely, everthreatened, farms in the Negev. The story of this radical change, bringing so many others in its wake, could doubtless be one of the keys of this book; but it has not been attempted as yet. It apparently began in Eastern Europe when the ghettoes experienced the effects of the French Revolution and of the pogroms at one and the same time. The Jewish intellectuals, in learning to fight beside the revolutionaries, for the Russian people who did not follow them, doubtless learned to fight for their own people who did not follow them either. But they discovered a liberty which none could destroy. Trumpeldor and Jabotinski, the first to symbolise Jewish courage, were both Russians. In God's eyes the revolutionary struggle was no less vain than any other, but there was a broad enough aura of religion about the Revolution to hide traditional concepts at times . . . In any case, Jewish communities probably suffered the same religious decay which affected the rest of Europe. A retreat from God was needed before the hero could at last confront Religion, so that the indomitable submission of Jewry could come to an end.

Yet God is still there and the Old Testament is the national literature of the State of Israel.

Hence springs the complex, endless argument so well conveyed by these photographs. The decisive transformation which guarantees the State's survival gives it no vital purpose; the Israeli army is like the revolutionary militia of an unknown revolution. The State is a nation in arms, the symbol of the radical change which has turned an intellectual and business community into a nation of peasant-soldiers, and yet the peasants of the kibbutz are like no other peasants, these fighters no ordinary soldiers, nor is the nation itself like the old nations of Europe, still less does it resemble the nations of America, the creations of uprooted energy. To the call of the Millenium this nation unites a ruthless rationalism, with the creation of a republic under Lord Balfour she mingles the return to a Promised Land under the Messiah. Her population of townsmen will not forget metaphysics as they master the plough, her people hardly less scourged by Justice than by God, will not forget it when she discovers her political rationale. Here—despite the disasters, despite the need to live as one nation—there is no continuity, and yet all is indissoluably linked to a past from which the Almighty has not yet been driven.

Overshadowing the problems of the pioneers (what captions are quite like those you will read under the pictures in this book?), the State of Israel is facing in the world of today precisely those problems that the new-born West had to meet in the eleventh century. Even if Western Christendom had gone under, she would still have given birth to the world she did create out of the other world with which she was obsessed. It is self-evident that neither is she the Gospel incarnate nor is the Soviet Union Marxism, nor

France of the year II the Republic, nor the State of Israel the Old Testament. But without the Gospel—or what the Gospel became—Western Christendom could never have existed, so neither could the State of Israel have come into being without the Old Testament, or rather what the Old Testament has become in the changes which have not stopped short of the sacred. If the underlying accent of these photographs exalts the spirit of those who build the State it gives expression, too, to the forces beneath the surface that now impede and now inspire it—the soul of the rabbi who preached submission to ensure the survival of Israel, and the heart of the sage who dies under torture to perpetuate its memory, and the mothers, sometimes for, sometimes against—forces which make the Zionist State, whether one likes it or not, the latest chapter of Israel's destiny. That destiny is not only history but also the timeless spirit of a Rembrandt night-piece, in which Alterman's two ghosts walk, and from which the sentry of the last page springs out.

The sun sets on the sands that will cover the Jewish State as they cover many others. "The morning cometh and also the night," says Isaiah. "Night cometh and also the morning" answers a black shape in the dusk. The mountains it guards have seen Jerusalem seventeen times destroyed. It watches over girls who dream of the serenade, "My beloved comes on the Sabbath—my mother slumbers, my father sleeps—only my heart and I are awake!" and in the shadow of Scheol, which grows darker as the Pleiades mount in the sky, the Judges of Israel look down on the tiny doomed sentinel against whom God's threats cannot prevail because the mystery of the dignity of the most lowly is no less profound than that of death.

ANDRE MALRAUX

If God had revealed the Law unto Israel in an inhabited country, that country would have become inflamed with pride and would have considered itself privileged among all the nations. Therefore, God revealed His Law in a desert. He revealed it in the

THE DESERT OF JUDAEA

desert in order to show that the children of the Law must be free even as the children of the desert. He revealed it in the desert above all to indicate that His Law is a common heritage.

(MIDRASH)

He (Moses) was the first to realise the astounding project of creating an united nation from a wretched handful of fugitives, uncivilised and unendowed, unarmed and unwarlike and unprepossessing, who without an inch of land to their name were wanderers on the face of the earth. Moses dared to build a free people bound by a code of law upon this band of escaped slaves. And while this people wandered in the desert without a stone on which to lay their heads Moses gave them institutions that have survived despite time, chance and conquest. Five thousand years have neither destroyed nor even altered them and they survive today in all their vigour although the nation itself has passed away.

JEAN-JACQUES ROUSSEAU
(1712–1778)

Moses presenting the Ten Commandments to the Children of Israel at the foot of Mount Sinai.
(From a fourteenth-century Haggadah: illuminated manuscript in the National Museum, Sarajevo.)

15

Bedouin children from a tribe in the Beersheba region. In the times of the Old Testament, the Hebrews lived much the same life on the plains of the Negev as do these semi-nomadic Bedouin today.

Travel in Judaea at first brings heart-searing boredom, but then, moving from one desert to another, boundless emptiness ever before you, the black mood passes, you become prey to a secret fear, a fear which far from depressing you, gives you courage and elevates your perceptions.   The fantastic scenery unveils a land everywhere moulded by the miraculous: the burning sunshine, the wheeling eagle, the barren fig trees: all the poetry, all the imagery of the Bible are there.   Every place-name enshrines its mystery, every cave foretells the future, every hill-top resounds with the voice of a prophet.   Here God Himself has spoken: the dried-up streams, the shattered rocks, the crumbling tombs witness the miracle.   The deserts still seem dumb with fear, as though having once heard the voice of the Almighty they have never since dared break silence.

CHATEAUBRIAND
(1768–1848)

Both left and right, there's only sand.
Yellowing sand over trackless land.
The caravan glides quietly by,

Like a wondrous dream it seems to fly.
Its music flows in rhythmic beat,
In desolate wastes tread camels' feet,

Lin lan, lin lan—a roving song,
Bear burdens dumbly, plod along.

JACOB FICHMAN

And Ruth the Moabitess said unto Naomi, Let me now go to the field, and glean ears of corn after him in whose sight I shall find grace. And she said unto her, Go my daughter.

And she went, and came, and gleaned in the field after the reapers: and her hap was to light on a part of the field belonging unto Boaz, who was of the kindred of Elimelech.

And, behold, Boaz came from Bethlehem, and said unto the reapers, The Lord be with you. And they answered him, The Lord bless thee.

Then said Boaz unto his servant that was set over the reapers, Whose damsel is this?

And the servant that was set over the reapers answered and said, It is the Moabitish damsel that came back with Naomi out of the country of Moab.

And she said, I pray you, let me glean and gather after the reapers among the sheaves: so she came, and hath continued even from the morning until now, that she tarried a little in the house.

Then said Boaz unto Ruth, Hearest thou not, my daughter? Go not to glean in another field, neither go from thence, but abide here fast by my maidens.

Let thine eyes be on the field that they do reap, and go thou after them: have I not charged the young men that they shall not touch thee? and when thou art athirst, go unto the vessels, and drink of that which the young men have drawn.

RUTH 2 : 2-9

The sun was risen upon the earth when Lot entered into Zoar. Then the Lord rained upon Sodom and upon Gomorrah brimstone and fire from the Lord out of heaven;

And he overthrew those cities, and all the plain, and all the inhabitants of the cities, and that which grew upon the ground.

But his wife looked back from behind him, and she became a pillar of salt.

GENESIS 19 : 23-26

SODOM—LOT'S WIFE

Vespasian reached the shore and ordered a number of men, who could not swim, to be thrown into the water. Their hands, too, were tied behind their backs, and yet they all bobbed up to the surface as though brought up from the depths by a bubble of air . . . In many places the Dead Sea casts up pieces of bitumen, in shape and size most like the headless bodies of cattle, and these black lumps float on its surface.

FLAVIUS JOSEPHUS
(37–100 A. D.)

THE DEAD SEA

My soul is weary of my life;
I will leave my complaint upon myself;
I will speak in the bitterness of my soul.
I will say unto God: Do not condemn me;
shew me wherefore thou contendest with me.
Is it good unto thee that thou shouldest oppress,
that thou shouldest despise the work of thine hands,
and shine upon the counsel of the wicked?
Hast thou eyes of flesh?
Or seeth thou as man seeth?
Are thy days as the days of man?
Are thy years as man's days,
That thou inquirest after mine iniquity,
and searchest after my sin?
Thou knowest that I am not wicked;
and there is none that can deliver out of thine hand.

JOB 10: 1-7

O thou seer, go, flee thee away into the land of Judah,
And there eat bread, and prophesy there.

AMOS 7: 12

Go flee! No! Such a man as I shall not retreat.
My flock taught me to step with gentle pace;
Nor has my tongue learned fear or base deceit,
My word shall fall as falls a heavy mace.

And if my strength is spent, 'tis not my wrong.
The sin is yours. Bear the iniquity!
My hammer found no anvil firm and strong,
My axe struck but the soft rot of a tree.

It matters not! I'll make peace with my fate
And to my girdle bind my tools, the same
As unpaid labourer when day grows late;
And then I'll leave as softly as I came,

Return to my own vales and habitat,
Make with the forest sycamores my stay,
But you, decaying mouldiness and rot,
Tomorrow's storm shall fling you far away.

CHIAM NACHMAN BIALIK
(1873-1934)

And he came down to Capernaum, a city of Galilee,
and taught them on the sabbath days.
And they were astonished at his doctrine: for his word
was with power.

LUKE 4: 31-32

Galilee still holds the remains of several ancient synagogues.

Inside they were equipped with benches, a pulpit for the reader and a cupboard in which were kept the sacred scrolls. These buildings—they were in no sense temples— were the centre of Jewish life. On every sabbath day there were gatherings for prayer and for readings of the Law and the Prophets. Since, outside Jerusalem, the Jewish faith was not administered by clergy, in our sense of the term, the earliest arrival would get up, read the passage of Scripture appropriate to the day, and then discuss it in his own terms, giving expression to his own ideas upon it. It was quite permissible for arguments and objections to be raised with the reader, and hence the meeting soon degenerated into a kind of debating club. There was a president, elders, the "chazan," the accredited reader or beadle, envoys who filled the positions of secretary and messenger between the various synagogues, and a shammis, or sacristan. In fact, the synagogues were really little independent republics.

Given the extraordinary intellectual agility of the Jew, such an institution, despite its arbitrary and essential limitations, was the scene of many hard-fought arguments. Thanks to its synagogues, Judaism has come safely through eighteen centuries of persecution, these synagogues being so many private little worlds which preserved the national traditions and offered the ideal floor for ventilating internal discords.

The freedom, offered to all who wished to take it, to step forward and read and comment upon the Scriptures afforded a wonderful opportunity to advance new interpretations of them. In this lay one of Jesus' mainsprings, and it was his usual method of establishing and teaching his doctrine. He would enter the synagogue and stand up to read. The chazan would hand him the scrolls which he would unroll and, in reading the set chapter for the day, would evolve from his reading an argument expressive of his ideas.

E. RENAN
(1823–1892)

THE SYNAGOGUE, CAPERNAUM (second or third century A.D.). Excavated from 1905 to 1926, it is the finest ancient synagogue in Galilee and perhaps in Israel and can be compared to the best pagan temples of the same period. Archeologists have attempted to restore this synagogue from the fragments of its destruction by an earthquake, but the work was interrupted by World War Two.

Step into their homes, you will find a people who, in the depths of grinding poverty, still teach their children to read a mysterious book, and in their turn those children will teach their children. As it was five thousand years ago so it is today. Seventeen times have they seen Jerusalem destroyed, but nothing can prevent their lifting up their eyes to Zion.

The Persians, the Greeks and the Romans have vanished from the earth but the stock of this small nation, coming to birth before the great nations, still continues unadulterated in the ruins of its native land. If in the life of peoples anything can be characterised as miraculous, this characteristic, we hold, must reside here.

CHATEAUBRIAND
(1768–1848)

Oh bring us home in peace from the four corners of the earth and lead us heads held high into our land.

Morning Prayer

JERUSALEM, STREET OF THE PROPHETS

THE SACRIFICE OF ISAAC (Fifth-century mosaic in the Synagogue of Beth-Alpha.)

Aphorisms from the Haggadah. The Haggadah was for many centuries the principal vehicle for Jewish literary forms: stories, fables, essays, riddles, parables, anecdotes as well as religious, social and political meditations. Based at first upon oral tradition, the Haggadah is part of the Talmud and was definitively edited at the end of the fourth century.

Man was created on the sixth day so that he could not be boastful, since he comes after the flea in the order of creation.

Once a pagan came to Shamai and asked him to teach him the Torah while standing on one leg. Shamai repulsed him. The tenacious pagan then went to Hillel with the same proposal. Hillel consented. "That which is hateful to you," he said to him, "do not impose upon others." This is the whole Torah, the rest is only commentary.

I have learned much from my teachers, and from my colleagues more than from my teachers, and from my students more than from all.

Greater is he who enjoys the fruit of his labour than he who fears heaven.

Where there are no men strive thou to be a man.

Four things impair the strength of man: sin, journeying, fasting and royalty.

It is written: "Our days on the earth are as a shadow." One consoles oneself by saying: Would that life were like the shadow cast by a wall or a tree, but is is like the shadow of a bird in flight.

RITUAL OBJECTS (Fifth-century mosaic from the Synagogue of Beth-Alpha)

A man said to the fruit trees: "Why does one not hear your voice?". They replied: "We have no such need; our fruits bear witness for us."

If a man says unto you: "I have sought and not found, do not believe; I have not sought and I have found, do not believe; I have sought and I have found" believe him.

Woman prefers poverty with love to luxury without it.

THE VALLEY OF ZEBULUN

If a man owes you money and he is unable to pay you, do not pass before him.

There are four minds in the bed of a divorced man who married a divorced woman.

Every man who does not teach his son a trade, it is as though he teaches him to rob.

There is no blessing greater than the blessing of peace.

(Aphorisms from the Haggadah)

And when the messengers of John were departed, he began to speak unto the people concerning John, What went ye out into the wilderness for to see? A reed shaken with the wind?

But what went ye out for to see? A prophet? Yea, I say unto you, and much more than a prophet.

This is he, of whom it is written, Behold, I send my messenger before thy face, which shall prepare thy way before thee.

For I say unto you, Among those that are born of women there is not a greater prophet than John...

LUKE 7 : 24-28

Monday, 2 April: Outside the walls of Jerusalem a Russian pilgrim was buried—so many die on the journey through Palestine. She was an old woman, her face, the colour of yellow wax, was exposed as she was carried to her grave by the other peasant women. Behind came pilgrims in their hundreds, men and women. A mass of worn skirts, fur caps, grey-bearded peasants, a dingy, dirty mob. But their faces were lit up by their triumphant faith and they sang a hymn of joy in unison. How lucky they considered her, how they envied her, for she had died in the Holy Land. Oh! The faith of those simple people.

P. LOTI
(1850–1923)

THE CHURCH OF ST. JOHN-THE-BAPTIST IN THE VILLAGE OF EIN KAREM, NEAR JERUSALEM

How from among all peoples
Was I plunged into an abyss?
And from the day I was delivered to devastation
Is there neither help nor rising?

Why are all my neighbours
Rebuilt from all of their ruins,
Whilst I these many years
Weep over two destructions?

AMITTAI ben SEFATYAH
(In Italy, circa 900)

And fields shall be bought in this land,

whereof ye say, It is desolate without man or beast;

it is given into the hand of the Chaldeans.

Men shall buy fields for money,

and subscribe evidences, and seal them,

and take witnesses

in the land of Benjamin, and in the places about Jerusalem,

and in the cities of Judah, and in the cities of the mountains,

and in the cities of the valley, and in the cities of the south:

for I will cause their captivity to return, saith the Lord.

JEREMIAH 52:43-44

An old man sits on a hill near Jerusalem and watches the planting of the Martyr's Forest, six million trees to preserve the memory of Hitler's victims.

JERUSALEM, YEAR 3000

Beautiful height. O joy! the whole world's gladness!
O great King's city, mountain blest!
My soul is yearning unto thee—is yearning
From limits of the west.

The torrents heave from depths of mine heart's passion,
At memory of thine olden state,
The glory of thee borne away to exile,
Thy dwelling desolate.

And who shall grant me, on the wings of eagles,
To rise and seek thee through the years,
Until I mingle with thy dust beloved,
The waters of my tears?

I seek thee, though thy King be no more in thee,
Though where the balm hath been of old—
Thy Gilead's balm—be poisonous adders lurking,
Winged scorpions manifold.

Shall I not to thy very stones be tender?
Shall I not kiss them verily?
Shall not thine earth upon my lips taste sweeter
Than honey unto me?

JUDAH HA-LEVI
(Cordoba, 1100–1150?)

JERUSALEM. The mediaeval fortifi-
cations of the Citadel. The towers
and ramparts date from the Crusades
and Mameluke times. In the background can be seen the minaret
known as "The Tower of David."

With every rolling stone place me in the breach
and strengthen me with hammers,
perhaps to appease my lord, that of sin
of the nation, who did not build the ruins may be pardoned.

How good to know, that I were a stone like all the stones of Jerusalem,
and how happy I should be if my bones were joined to the wall,
that my body might be no poorer than my soul, which shouting or silent,
went through fire and water with the nation.

Take me with the Jerusalem stone and place me in the walls
and press me in with plaster,
and from their strength my bones will sing, that pine
to greet the Messiah.

JUDAH KARNI

By the rivers of Babylon, there we sat down, yea, we wept, when we remembered Zion.

We hanged our harps upon the willows in the midst thereof.

For there they that carried us away captive required of us a song; and they that wasted us required of us mirth, saying, Sing us one of the songs of Zion.

How shall we sing the Lord's song in a strange land?

If I forget thee, O Jerusalem, let my right hand forget her cunning.

If I do not remember thee, let my tongue cleave to the roof of my mouth; if I prefer not Jerusalem above my chief joy.

PSALMS 137: 1-6

PARABLES FROM THE HAGGADAH

Rabbi Samuel was visiting Rome. One day he found in the street some jewels of great value. While he was admiring them a public crier announced that the queen had lost her jewels (which corresponded to those picked up by Rabbi Samuel) and if the jewels were returned within a given time of 30 days a reward would be offered. He who procrastinated until the lapse of 30 days would have his head cut off. Rabbi Samuel did exactly the opposite. He waited until the prescribed period had elapsed before presenting himself to the court. "Didn't you hear my announcement?" the queen asked.
"Of course," answered Rabbi Samuel. "But why did you disobey?" "In order to show you that it is from fear of God, the most holy blessed be He, and not fear of you, that I return your property to you.

One day Rabbi Eleazar the son of Simon showed a Roman officer of the law whose duty it was to seek and arrest thieves, how he might apprehend them in such a way as not to catch the innocent.

"Visit the inns," he said to him, "at 10 o'clock during the morning. If you see a man half asleep, a glass of wine in his hand, inquire about him. If he is a scholar or a night-worker, then he sleeps thus because he rose early. If he is neither the one nor the other, arrest him, he is a thief."

The king, learning of this, ordered that the author of the plan be responsible for carrying it out. Named chief of police, Rabbi Eleazar, from the moment he assumed this office, arrested many thieves using, of course, his own methods.

Rabbi Joshua, learning of Rabbi Eleazar's vocation, was shocked. He sent to him saying: "How long will you continue to deliver the people of God to their death?"
"I but weed the thorns from the vines," answered Rabbi Eleazar.
To which Rabbi Joshua answered: "Let the owner of the vineyard destroy the thorns himself."

SAFED

ISRAEL, LAND OF THE BIBLE

No, you won't dive into the past along this road, you'll climb into it. This road is a climb, leading... but where does it lead to? Let's fix its starting-point first: from sea level from the seventy-five miles of coast line along the inland sea in whose waves are reflected the Pyramids, the Acropolis, the Coliseum, Notre-Dame de la Garde and which come to die in the port of Jaffa (don't disturb the man asleep in the hold of that ship: he is Jonah, the prophet: he flees the Call); or from even lower down, for, while still remaining in the State, you were perhaps in that deep valley the Jordan has carved out for herself as she flows towards the choking salt lake 1150 feet below sea level (don't wake the woman dreaming on the frontier: she is Ruth: she has come from Moab to glean the fields of Bethlehem). Such are the depths from which begins the road which leads, from whichever point you set out, but where does it lead? One thing alone is certain: the road climbs upwards. We must climb with it, and it never ceases to mount higher and higher in dizzying hairpin bends up the flank of the foot-hills up the mountains and at every corner comes a fresh view, a single view: the need to mount still higher. And added to the knowledge that we cannot escape from the struggle of the climb is a delirious feeling, a feeling of mystery. At each corner it closes in on us, wrapping itself more closely around us, as though to forewarn us of what will be suddenly revealed in the final ravine that rends the landscape in two. The first landscape is the one to which we have become so used after hours of dogged travel; the other, quite different, quite breath-taking, shapes itself in new forms and fresh colours. No more the perspective of hills rising piled one above the other but the last slope; a peak; the summit; and perched on it the tower. We must still climb to reach it, but it is there, held out to our eyes at every corner. It is held out to us like the mystery, the promise, the distant shining future of our brightest dreams, because we must await their realisation, and of the greatest moments of our life, because hope swells them. But it is towards the past that we journey, the past revered, august, majestic, formalised in the countless holy pictures adored by millions of the faithful, the past concentrated into four hieratic syllables: JERUSALEM. Yes the road

leads to Jerusalem (do not disturb God, when you hear the rise and fall of His breathing beside the Wailing Wall, at the Holy Sepulchre, in the Mosque of the Caliph, or in the countless other places, beneath the olive-trees, in some street, in the shade of some tower). But it was not the venerable Tower of David that you saw from the distance, that tower was one of the countless Israeli buildings that sprung up yesterday, and will spring up tomorrow and which are, none-the-less the sign of fixity, change, and survival amid the whirl of the centuries.

I recognise the rise and fall of peoples. Some disappeared in the far-off age which lies heavily upon them. Their dust is no more than a thin layer in the earth's crust and one must delve with the patience of the archeologist, dig and delve to catch a fleeting glimpse of them. Sometimes something marvellous is revealed, always something lifeless. In this way the dust has been cleared from the Sumerians and the Hittites, but no spirit will ever call them back to life. A different fate has befallen others. More astonishingly they live, have never ceased to live, they step across the pages of history and yet their sun has set. At some historic moment the thunder-stroke has marked them and they have been, as it were, split asunder. Now they remember two separate lives, the old life, now finished in their eyes, and the new life that the thunder flash called into being which they see as the true life. They are the heirs of two traditions in sacramental contradiction the one to the other, in conscious and unavoidable contradiction. If you have visited Egypt, Greece or Italy, as I have, then you will recognise such peoples, inhabiting a country and yet sharing neither its destiny nor its past. The way of life and the monuments we admire are of another age, one with which the inhabitants have broken completely. Christianity or Islam has smitten them, withered them up, converted them and cut them off from the source of their being. Between them and their beginnings is a great gulf, the change from the death of paganism to the birth of monotheism. They are at odds with the monuments of the past from which they were converted and among which they live. They do not speak the same language, theirs is an alien spirit. Such peoples look proudly on what they deny every day in their heart of hearts. They are museum attendants, grave watchers.

Israel is an unconverted people, the only one in our Western and Middle Eastern civilisation, may I say our Biblical civilisation. There is no break, no recantation in their history. Two thousand years ago the diaspora forced them to leave their native land and scattered them to the four quarters of the globe, but the Spirit of their country never left them. In the course of those two thousand years they were forced to learn the tongues of seventy nations, but they never forgot the language of the Old Testament. They were compelled to walk on the fringes of every civilisation in the world but the intuition of their own culture never left them. An unbroken chain of prayer, in the language of the Old Testament, addressed to the land of the Old Testament, links the last Jewish emigrant in the reign of Titus to the first Jewish immigrant in Tzarist times.

There is something more than merely place to join the Israeli of the twentieth century to the Hebrew of antiquity, there is a common destiny.

The man asleep in the bottom of the hold really was Jonah; the woman gleaning the field really was Ruth, and the God dozing by the Wailing Wall was the true God. Together they shake off their sleep and here everyone recognises them, greets them with a depth of feeling, but not of astonishment, just as one would greet the brother who steps quickly and firmly into the joy of a reunited family. God, the prophet, and the gleaner spread about them the atmosphere of brotherly love among the nation that speaks their language, is filled with their Spirit, and partakes of the mysterious yet real intimacy of a shared vocation. The realisation that in no other country are the holy places objects of such intense veneration is the realisation that they are holy not only in place but in time. Their unbroken connection with Old Testament times is the living unbroken history of the people of the Old Testament. Rome and Mecca are fortresses in conquered territory —their foundation stones are pagan—but since Abraham spoke with Melchizedek, since David wrote the Psalms, the people of the Old Testament have lived in Jerusalem. In this land of Israel if you notice a particular cast of countenance or of thought, a name, a place, a course of conduct, it is not a mere momentary echo of poetry or of folklore but the recapturing of the permanence of Old Testament life in the swift passage of time. The organisation of the kibbutz is Old Testament justice. Landed property held in common is Old Testament ethics. The reclamation of the desert is an Old Testament promise. The road along which we travel to thy past, O Jerusalem, now hedged with a future of as many trees as victims burned on Auschwitz and the other altars, is the destiny of the Old Testament. Finally thy name, O Israel, which the Angel gave thee in the night when thou didst wrestle for God, and in which are linked for eternity God and the man who was prepared to fight for him, as if a shaft of light divine illumined the purpose of the life in all its petty detail, thy name is the presence and the perennity of the Old Testament.

ANDRÉ NEHER

The hand of the Lord was upon me, and carried me out in the spirit of the Lord, and set me down in the midst of the valley which was full of bones. And caused me to pass by them round about: and, behold there were very many in the open valley and, lo, they were very dry. And he said unto me, Son of man, can these bones live? And I answered, O Lord God, thou knowest. Again he said unto me, Prophesy upon these bones, and say unto them, O ye dry bones, hear the word of the Lord. Thus saith the Lord God unto these bones; Behold, I will cause breath to enter into you, and ye shall live: And

Amsterdam, *Friday, May 26, 1944.*

"Again and again I ask myself, would it not have been better for us all if we had not gone into hiding, and if we were dead now and not going through all this misery, especially as we should no longer be dragging our protectors into danger. But we all recoil from these thoughts too, for we still love life; we haven't yet forgotten the voice of nature, we still hope, hope about everything."

Tuesday, June 6, 1944.

"...The best part of the invasion is that I have the feeling that friends are approaching. We have been oppressed by those terrible Germans for so long, they have had their knives so at our throats, that the thought of friends and delivery fills us with confidence!

"...Perhaps, Margot says, I may yet be able to go back to school in September or October."

ANNE FRANK
"The Diary of a Young Girl"

On the outskirts of Jerusalem Israeli children take part in planting the Martyr's Forest, in memory of Hitler's victims.

will lay sinews upon you, and will bring up flesh upon you, and cover you with skin, and put breath in you, and ye shall live ; and ye shall know that I am the Lord.   So I prophesied as I was commanded : and as I prophesied, there was a noise, and behold a shaking, and the bones came together, bone to his bone.   And when I beheld, lo, the sinews and the flesh came up upon them, and the skin covered them above : and there was no breath in them.   Then he said unto me, Prophesy unto the wind, prophesy, Son of man and say to the wind, Thus saith the Lord God : Come from the four winds, O breath,

and breathe upon these slain, that they may live. So I prophesied as he commanded me, and the breath came into them, and they lived, and stood up upon their feet, an exceeding great army. Then he said unto me, Son of man, these bones are the whole house of Israel: behold, they say, Our bones are dried, and our hope is lost: we are cut off for our parts. Therefore prophesy and say unto them, Thus saith the Lord God; Behold, O my people, I will open your graves, and cause you to come up out of your graves, and bring you into the land of Israel.

EZEKIEL 37:1-12

The British Government announced: "No steps will be taken to assist the passage of Jewish refugees to Palestine."

And the sky glowed red above Auschwitz.

And they were fighting for the freedom of the world.

February 24, 1942, is, in fact, a stain on British history. The *Strouma* had been tied up in Istambul for two months awaiting visas for Palestine. When finally it was decided to permit the entry of the children, the Turkish authorities had already sent the vessel back to the Black Sea. It foundered. There were 764 men and women aboard. There was one survivor.

F.-J. ARMORIN

Dinner hour for the workmen who are building the new road which will link Beersheba and Sodom. Starting from the capital of the Negev and ending on the shores of the Dead Sea, its highest point is 1312 feet above and its lowest 1279 feet below sea level.

And the parched ground shall become a pool,
and the thirsty land springs of water:
in the habitation of dragons,
where each lay, shall be grass
with reeds and rushes.
And a highway shall be there, and a way...

Prepare ye the way
of the people;
cast up the highway;
gather out the stones...

       ISAIAH 35 : 7-8 and 62 : 10

Building the road from Beersheba, capital of the Negev, to Sodom: in the background, the Dead Sea and the Mountains of Edom.

THE EXODUS FROM YEMEN

Yemen lies in the south-west corner of the Arabian peninsular. Among its million inhabitants were 40,000 Jews. This nation within a nation preserved its first innocence, having had very little contact with outside civilisation for the past twelve centuries. The Jewish community in Yemen was probably the oldest in the world, traditionally founded during the reign of King Solomon, but possibly after the capture of Jerusalem by the Babylonians in 587 B.C. The foundation of the State of Israel seemed to them to usher in the age of the Messiah. The exodus from Yemen began. A shuttle-service of six giant Skymasters carried them to Israel; this was *Operation Magic Carpet*.

Here the exodus of 1949 is described by a Yemenite.

We dwelt in exile and awaited the Redemption without realising that it would come. One of us went up to the capital and returned and told us: "The State of Israel exists." But we did not know whether the thing he said was true. Day succeeded day and we were given neither word nor sign. None-the-less, last year, the rumours increased and men came to us from afar who said, "There is a King in Israel." And in a little while, "There is an army in Israel, an army of heroes." At last they told us saying, "These are the dreadful things that herald the Messiah, for there is war in Israel." And we remained in exile knowing not whether these things were true. We hoped for the Redemption but our spirit grew restless. And we threw off our exile and it was as though the spirit of God was in us and exhorted us saying, "Come with me and let us go up into the Land of Israel." But we still asked, "Is there news of the Redemption?" and they answered us, "Be patient. The prophecies will be realised in due time"... And many of us had already packed our belongings and waited the sign that never came, until lo, a letter reached us in which it was written. "Awake, my brethren, rise up. The hour has come. Our land, for her Redemption and for yours, awaits her children to rebuild the ruined places. Overcome the sufferings and hardships of the journey, for without you Israel will not be redeemed. Take heart and set out on the instant, but take with you the Scrolls of the Law

and your garments, the symbols of the antiquity of our people."

... And we went to the synagogue and there we prayed for our dead asking pardon and oblivion, for we knew that the Land of Israel signified the remission of sin and that our fathers would forgive us. And we took up the Scrolls of the Law and the holy things to carry them into our land. But often the holy books and the Scrolls of the Law were buried for they could not be taken. And we made ready food for our journey, each family food for itself, bread and rancid butter, dried meat, spices and coffee. And we carried with us flour for the journey, and the women gathered twigs and made fires in empty tins in the open. So they made us bread or wrapped the dough around stones and set them on the fire.

But the frontier was closed because we were so many and we were compelled to encamp here and there. We prayed with a special fervour, our hearts were broken and our tears bedewed the ground. When should we be worthy to cross the threshold?

Then came the day when famine threatened to destroy us and there was no bread for our mouths. And when we thought of our children our hearts were riven. Then we arose and prayed unto the Lord and the Almighty heard us. And even as we prayed came Arabs bringing food and saying, "Give us of your silver and you shall have bread."

And many of us fell ill on the journey and there was neither medicine nor physician nor even so much as a drop of milk to save the children . . . And there were women carried on the backs of asses and when their time came they bore their children as they rode along, and mothers and babies were on the backs of asses. And one day a messenger came from Israel and spoke with us and encouraged our hearts and filled us with the breath of life.

For he said to us, "Have no fear for none shall remain in exile in Yemen, and the State of Israel shall not leave you helpless . . ." And he kept the promise he had made.

Parties came from every part of the Yemen and our hearts yearned within our breasts so great was our desire to see the Land of Israel. Thus we came unto Aden, at the last gasp, beaten and robbed, weak, our possessions taken from us. And we had been on the road for two months and some of us three. We were assembled in a great camp near the town. It stretched among the sands of the desert but it was too small for our numbers, so that we lay down family by family upon the very sands and the sky was our roof. Then terrible sand storms raged and in our hearts we prayed for our going up into Israel.

"Oh for the wings of the eagle to carry us into our native land."

And we were taken up into the air.

THE PROPHET ELIJAH ANNOUNCES THE COMING OF THE MESSIAH
(From an illuminated Haggadah Manuscript, 1752, in the private Collection of V. Klagsbald, Paris.)

A Yemenite family brought to Israel by "Operation Magic Carpet" and lodged in a *maabarah* (temporary camp). They will soon be transferred to a new farm settlement. The Yemenites speak Hebrew perfectly, they are rooted in the traditions and customs of Israel and are good farmers. They have only to master modern machinery and methods to become a basic element in the rebirth of Israel.

MAABARAH. The immigrants are at first housed in temporary camps. These camps are situated near development projects, and the people in them are found suitable employment which enables them to fit easily into the life of the country. Then, too, it is near such sites that the immigrants' permanent homes are built. In this way, once the houses are built they leave the temporary camps (called, in Hebrew, *maabarah*) for their permanent homes.

A garden have I, and also a well
And in my well there is a bucket.
My beloved comes on the sabbath,
To drink clear water from my cup.

The whole universe is sleeping.   Hush!
The apple and the pear nod.
My mother slumbers, my father sleeps,
Only my heart and I are awake.

CH. N. BIALIK
(1873–1934)

This girl has only just arrived in Israel. She is engaged in raffia work in one of the workshops in the *maabarah*. She will go on with this work when she has settled into the village which is being built beside the temporary camp. Thus, from the moment she lands she takes her place in the economic life of the country.

Hodja Nour had become the darling of the settlement. Everyone loved him. In moments of danger all eyes turned to him. Should a settler take sick Hodja would jump on his horse in all haste and rush to the neighbouring settlement to fetch the doctor. He was the first to run after the Arab shepherds who came to plunder their vineyards, and he was the first to come out when the alarm was sounded.

The Arabs loved him too for his courage, his eloquence and his chivalry. They took part, more than once, in the races he organised. On horseback he would attire himself in their manner. Like them he would be armed from head to toe: and they bestowed their highest praise upon him by saying, "He is like us: an Arab."

One of the things about him they appreciated most was his hospitality. No one else in the settlement knew how to receive as he did according to the strictest code of the Orient. Should a sheik be passing by, he would immediately ask for the address of Hodja Nour. Even the Bedouins who came from afar had heard of him. Occasionally, he would sacrifice a kid in their honour. He had so high a reputation for integrity that peasants from neighbouring villages would seek him out to arbitrate their disputes.

Young Arab girls loved him too. At times, during the summer, when he was guarding the vineyards at night, some dark-eyed young Bedouin girl from a nearby tent would slip into his hut. A bright fire shone in the young girl's eyes: her heart was beating so! And he would whistle, a sign of happiness: and his whistling would rend the silence of the night reaching me in my hut in the vineyards: I knew what it meant, and I envied my friend.

MOSHE SMILANSKI
(1874–1953)

Mounted sentry on a frontier kibbutz. Eternal vigilance is needed, for the frontier is so close and so long, and raids by Arab infiltrators so frequent.

Arab girl from the village of Abu Gosh on the barren uplands of Judaea. Hers is one of the Arab villages that has always maintained friendly relations with the pioneers of the State of Israel.

The story I shall tell took place in one of the villages around the holy city of Hebron. It happened a long time ago.

It was seed-time when the moon in the heavens is like a reaping-hook that has served twelve good years' harvests. Day was just breaking and the village awoke. The cocks had greeted the sun and, their duty done, were now silent.

It was then that the sheik's wife Miriam remembered that one of the stones of her handmill was broken and, taking a handful of wheat and rye, she went to her neighbour's hovel to grind her corn. As she went on her way she came upon her neighbour's daughter Latifah, a girl she could never bring herself to like, sitting beside her grindstone. Latifah was sitting, one leg tucked under her, one leg stretched before her, and her movements were graceful as she worked. As she busied herself at the grindstone, she sang sadly and nostalgically. Her eyes seemed to watch the turning stone, but she was far from her task of grinding the corn. She seemed to dream, and who can tell what dreams the heart of a young girl holds!

"Blessed be you this day, my daughter, may the peace of Allah be in your heart and may he guide you in the way you should go. One of my grindstones is broken, and I have come to you to grind my corn. I wish to make ready the loaves for my husband who goes to his fields—may Allah bless the work of his plough."

The girl did not answer but went on singing sadly. The only sound in the village was her song, for the women had ground their corn and all the grindstones were silent. The loaves had already been taken from the ovens, but Latifah's task was unfinished. Her basket was full of corn, and her sad song was endless.

The young men stood holding their loaves, their ploughshares across their shoulders, but their hearts were far from the work of the fields. They stood in silence, captivated by Latifah's song.

Then Miriam remembered why she had come there. She saw that her corn was unground, that her husband's loaves were unbaked; she saw too that the young men standing on the pathway were unwilling to leave the village. Then she noticed that as they kept time with Latifah's song they poured corn into her basket, grain after grain after grain.

Then a curse rose unbidden to Miriam's lips: "May the stones with which you grind clamp into your back!"

It was the stroke of doom. Miriam still spoke, but Latifah fell silent. The grindstones slid towards her, clamped into her back, and they remained forever immovable.

In this manner the tortoise was born.

Arab legend

Yemenite girl kneading dough beside Lake Tiberias. She is the heir of a family tradition: two thousand years ago, the Jewish housewife prepared her loaves in precisely the same way.

Jaffa or Yaffa, the Joppa of the Scriptures, is one of the oldest and most famous ports in the world. Pliny mentions it as one of the cities that stood before the flood. Tradition relates that it was here that Andromeda was chained to the rock as an offering to the sea monster; it was there that Noah built the Ark; and it was there that, by the order of King Solomon, were landed the cedars of Lebanon for the building of the Temple. Eighteen hundred and sixty-two years before Christ the prophet Jonah took ship from there. At the time of the Crusades, St. Louis fortified the town. In 1799, Bonaparte took it by assault and massacred his Turkish prisoners. It has a wretched port fit only for coasting vessels . . .

LAMARTINE
(1790–1869)

The builders of Tel Aviv originally only intended a holiday resort, where, after the day's work, a man could find quiet relaxation and where in the clean air the children could escape eyesores and other local diseases . . . gradually the scope of their plans widened, and they planned to build a permanent suburb in which people could live all the year round, summer and winter alike. About sixty persons formed a private company . . . They were in general agreement upon building the new suburb at a reasonable distance from the town of Jaffa. They each subscribed a small sum for initial expenses and the search for a site was begun. One was discovered in the sand dunes around the city . . . The land they bought consisted of sand dunes, flats and hollows. The hills were levelled and the sand was used to fill the hollows. Rocks were brought up from the sea and buried in the earth. Drains were dug. An endless line of camels and donkeys carried sand. Hammers banged and wheel-barrows were on the move . . . And now a causeway could be seen springing from the sand, a causeway firm beneath the foot. The population of Jaffa, men, women and children came out to try it. They thought it was a miracle. It did not crumble and their feet did not sink in the sand.

After S. Y. AGNON

TEL AVIV. THE BEACH WITH THE PORT OF JAFFA IN THE BACKGROUND

Building the largest hospital in Israel at Petah Tikvah.

In the heart of the desert Beersheba's ceaseless growth brings it to the verge of being a large town.

IN UPPER GALILEE

Friday evening. All work ends for this member of a religious co-operative village, and he returns home for his sabbath day of rest.

SAFED: 2789 feet above sea level and the most important town in Upper Galilee. In the days of the Hebrew kingdom it was one of the posting stations from which messages from Jerusalem proclaiming the new moon were passed. In the sixteenth century it was settled by Spanish Jews and many famous Cabalists lived there. Today its magnificent scenery makes it a favourite resort of painters and tourists.

From Safed I come, from Safed I come.
The winds, the hills, the nights
Give me these dark eyes.
The skies of the Galil and the waters of Miron
Make my eyes dreamy.
That's how we are,
That's what we are,
And I more than all—I am like that.
I come from Safed, I come from Safed.

NATHAN ALTERMAN

About this time Herod finished building Caesarea Sebasta. The whole was undertaken in ten years and the date for its completion fixed for the twenty-eighth year of his reign, in the hundred and ninety-second Olympiad. A solemn festival of dedication was proclaimed and was prepared at vast expense. The king announced a poetry competition and athletic games. He had collected a vast number of gladiators and wild beasts, there were to be horse races, and quantities of the most costly decorations had been brought from Rome and other lands. He dedicated the games to the emperor and determined to hold them every four years thereafter. The emperor defrayed the entire cost of the ceremonies from his privy purse so as to raise to yet greater heights the pomp of his reputation. In addition, the Empress Julia sent from her own treasury many of those things most highly esteemed in her country, so that the total expense amounted to no less than five hundred talents. Since a great crowd was drawn to the town for the games as well as embassies from those people who wished to acknowledge the privileges they had received from Herod, he welcomed them all, lodged them, kept open table for them and provided them with continual entertainments. By day they had the games, and at night shows so lavish that his generosity became a byword.

In fact he strove in all he did to surpass the splendour of the past.

It is even said that the emperor and Agrippa often remarked that his magnificence outran his power and that to have acted thus he should have been king of all Syria and Egypt.

FLAVIUS JOSEPHUS
(37–100 A.D.)

CAESAREA, Herod's ancient and splendid capital now has not one single inhabitant.

LAMARTINE
(1790–1869)

David Diasporin (unlike myself) was happy from the day he arrived in Israel. He had set himself the joyous two-fold task of merging with the Hebrew life of his environment and freeing himself from the yoke of his past in foreign lands which weighed upon him. Here, to him, all was new and free. He enjoyed walking around without a collar and going barefoot was his greatest pleasure. "Here we go barefoot as Hebrews," he liked to say humorously. Working was no hardship for this young man as it had proved to be for his old uncle and his elderly friend from the very first day they had arrived. Work? For him it was mere play. On holidays he would forget everything and abandon himself wholly to rest. He would forget Russia, Galicia and America . . . All around him were mountains, fields and the smell of nature. No problems, no metaphysics. He liked to walk alone, going from place to place, with joy in his heart. He would tell me how he had "returned to his mother's womb" while lying on the scorched grass and gazing at the flowers that never faded. Nevertheless I knew—and it hurt me—that the flowers, the real flowers would one day lose their perfume and that the idyl would come to an end.

J. CH. BRENNER
(1881–1921)

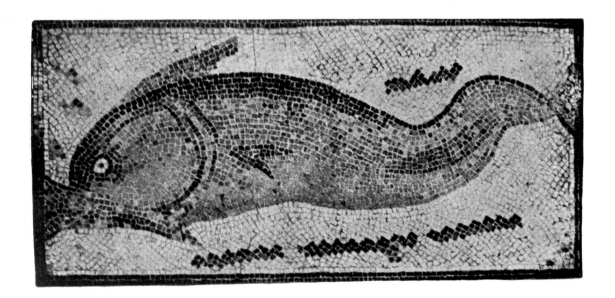

CAESAREA. For five hundred years the site of this town was abandoned. In 1940 some young Israelis with a few young immigrants established a fisherman's and farmers' co-operative on the site of the former port. They called the kibbutz S'Doth Yam (Fields of the Sea). The little colony played a major role in supporting illegal immigration in the face of the mandatory power. Today Caesarea is a centre of intensive agriculture and a large fishing port with a Nautical Training School Moaz-Yam (The Fortress of the Sea).

THE UPLANDS OF CARMEL. Several thousand Druses live among the uplands of Carmel. Their mythic-ancestor is Jethro (Moses' father-in-law) and therefore they consider themselves as cousins to the Hebrews. They never left their land and fought on the Israeli side in the War of Liberation in 1948. They form a minority of fifteen thousand duly recognised by Israel. On the uplands of Carmel is the "place of burning" where Elijah's contest with the priests of Baal took place. (I Kings 18.)

LYDDA

ON THE ROAD TO HAIFA

The world is an angry sea
Deep and wide,
And time is a frail bridge
Built across it.
At one end the bridge rises
From the coils of that which is not
Which preceded its being,
The other leads to everlasting grace
Shining in the light of His countenance.
The bridge is but as
The length of a man's arm.
No rails guard its sides
And you, son of man, perforce do you live
And you cross it without let
From the day you are born.
When you view the briefness of the road
Without chance to veer right or left,
Will you then boast of your glory and power?
When you glimpse devastation death bars your way
From the right and from the left
Will your heart stand firm—will your hands be strengthened?
And when you revel in the pride of possession
And in many things
Which you have accumulated thru sheer strength
And whose pursuit was your wish
Will you be caught in your own snare?
What will you do when the sea rages and roars
When it storms and rushes by
And your home too
Is threatened with destruction?

YEDAYAH HA-PENINI
(circa 1230–1240)

I behold graves of ancient time, of days long past,
Wherein a people sleeps the eternal sleep.
There is no enmity among these folk—no envy;
No loving of neighbour and no hating;
And my thought, envisioning them, cannot discern
Master from slave!

MOSES IBN EZRA
(Granada, 1070–1138)

It is well known that there is none of the harshness of Judaea in Galilee. In the spring-time the slopes are covered with those thousands of flowers from which Christ drew matter for many of his parables.

JACQUES MADAULE

THE HILLS OF NAZARETH

...You have chosen, you have made your choice and you have taken from among them the long lineage, rising ever to greater heights, the lofty mounting lineage of the prophets. And like the last crest of all, the last of the prophets—the first of the saints—stands Jesus, and he was a Jew.

... He was a Jew, an ordinary Jew, a Jew like you, a Jew among you. You knew him as well as the man of whom one says: "I used to know old so-and-so..." You saw the colour of his eyes; you heard the sound of his voice. Of the same lineage, for ever and ever.

CH. PEGUY
(1873–1914)

And he began again to teach by the sea side; and there was gathered unto him a great multitude, so that he entered into a ship, and sat in the sea; and the whole multitude was by the sea on the land. And he taught them many things by parables...

MARK 4: 1-2

CAPERNAUM (Hebrew: *Kfar Nahum*) is not mentioned in the Old Testament. Flavius Josephus knew it as *Capharnomum* and the Talmud as *Kefar Tanhum* (Place of Consolation). Capernaum was probably a frontier and customs post, where the great caravan route crossed a ford over the Jordan. Jesus stayed at Capernaum and made it the centre of his messianic work (Matt. 4: 13-17). The site of the majority of his miracles and of his parables is Capernaum on the shores of Lake Tiberias.

After these things Jesus shewed himself again to the disciples at the sea of Tiberias; and on this wise shewed he himself.

There were together Simon Peter, and Thomas called Didymus, and Nathanael of Cana in Galilee, and the sons of Zebedee, and two other of his disciples. Simon Peter saith unto them, I go a-fishing. They say unto him, We also go with thee. They went forth, and entered into a ship immediately, and that night they caught nothing. But when the morning was now come, Jesus stood on the shore : but the disciples knew not that it was Jesus. Then Jesus saith unto them, Children, have ye any meat? They answered him, No. And he said unto them, Cast the net on the right side of the ship, and ye shall find. They cast therefore, and now they were not able to draw it for the multitude of fishes.

JOHN 21 : 1-6

The valley of Ginossar is broad, rich and fertile, bounded by the rocky hills and lapped by the waters of Kinereth, as they call Lake Tiberias.

Gnarled countrymen and hardy fishers lived in this plain. They returned from exile in Babylon with Ezra and Nehemiah. First they helped to rebuild the ruins of Jerusalem, and then they set out to explore Galilee. They settled in the valley of Ginossar beside the waters of Kinereth, and their children carried on their parents' work so that what was once a ruined waste became a flowering garden.

Among the pioneers in the valley there was a man, renowned for his courage, who turned his back on the vineyards and the orchards and, choosing the waters of Kinereth,

THE VALLEY OF GINOSSAR

became a fisherman. He loved the lake for he knew all its secrets, by day and at night, in calm and in storm. The lake, his boat and his nets were his kingdom.

One day Herod led his armies into the valley. From his kingly tent he gazed out over the vineyards and the orchards that fell away to the blue waters of Kinereth. "What a marvellous spot," he exclaimed, "to build a resort for my servants."

So at once he called the people of the valley together and announced in sugared words: "I have taken pity upon you and I shall give you houses and lands in a place I shall choose for you. At dawn tomorrow you must leave this valley for I wish to build a new town as a resort for my servants."

The oldest fisherman, who had seven sons, all fishermen, spoke out to the king: "I, my father, my grandfather and my ancestors who returned from the Captivity, have lived here, and we love Kinereth. We shall not leave the valley though we die for it." As he spoke his face grew dark and troubled as the waters of Kinereth in the autumn storms.

At dawn Herod sent out his messengers to discover if his orders had been obeyed, but not one of them returned. He sent out others but they met the same fate. Then there was war between the army of Herod and the people of Ginossar who took refuge in caves and clefts in the rocks. So Herod ordered the trees and the bushes to be set on fire. The flames quickly took hold and reached the caves and consumed their defenders. Only the fisherman and his seven sons escaped.

The fisherman gathered his sons together and said, "I will not have us fall into the hands of Herod. Our brethren are dead, why should we live on in shame? Let us go and launch our boat upon Kinereth, the waters will welcome us in their mercy."

Without a word his seven sons followed the old fisherman. The waters were rough. They cast a last look upon the ruined valley, cut the moorings and made off among the tossing waves. Herod's men reached the shore too late to seize the fishermen. They saw the boat pitch and disappear beneath the waves, the old fisherman standing with his seven sons around him. There was a terrible crash of thunder, a flash of lightning rent the heavens and Kinereth seemed to cry aloud in anger.

Centuries have passed. Kinereth still laps against the grassy shores. But there are nights when the wind suddenly rises and whips up the waters. Then it is said that the voices of the old fisherman and his seven sons can be heard and their figures seen to rise above the crests of the foaming waves. Then no boat should venture out upon the waters of Kinereth, for Kinereth has not forgiven the slaughter of her farmers and the death of the men who cast their nets into her waters.

DAVID COHEN

THE FISHING VILLAGE OF EINGEV ON THE SHORES OF LAKE TIBERIAS

ST.-JEAN-D'ACRE. The names of such men as Richard Cœur-de-Lion, St. Louis, Saladin and Bonaparte have made the town famous. European immigrants occupy the new town, but the old still retains all its Oriental picturesqueness.

No State is handed over to a people
on a silver platter.
CH. WEIZMANN

. . . So the land grows still.   Red fades in the sky
Over the smoking frontiers in Israel.
Heartsick but breathing, the people greet
The wonder that has no parallel.

Beneath the moon, they stand and wait,
Facing the dawn in awe and joy;
Then slowly towards the waiting throng
Two step forth—a girl and a boy.

Clad for work and for war, heavy-shod and still,
Up the winding path they make their way,
Their clothes unchanged, still soiled with the grime
Of the battle-filled night and the toilsome day.

Weary past telling, strangers to sleep,
But wearing their youth like dew in their hair,
Dumb they approach.   Are they living or dead?
Who knows, as they stand unmoving there.

Tear-stained, wondering, the people ask,
"Who are you?"—Softly reply the two,
"We are the silver platter, on which
The Jewish State is handed you!"

In shadow they fall when their tale is told—
The rest let Israel's story unfold.

NATHAN ALTERMAN

These young men are training to build new collective
farms and learning to use their arms to defend their lands.
They are members of Nahal (The Young Pioneers' Army).

You can tell the extent of Jewish influence by the number of trees, and from when that influence dates by their height. A forestry map of Palestine would best express this argument. Unfortunately, however, during the war these same forests made ambushes all too easy and not only trees but wrecked vehicles lined the roadside during that heroic period when Jerusalem had to be supplied at all costs.

JACQUES MADAULE

Jerusalem is begirt with mountains,
with golden foundations and crowned with gold,
for there God's seers once walked,
Levites strode in glory,
and their tread was of nobles, like sleep-walkers
in the holy service.

And should a traveller stray in their paths
and smell of the stones that are scattered
like the bones in the valley of Ezekiel,
he will feel in his nostrils the incense of life—
and, drunk, he will prophesy:

"Stone joined to stone hewn for the house,
house joined to house for the beauty of quarters,
and I shall bequarter Jerusalem—
Jerusalem begirt with quarters."

How are the lovely quarters ravaged,
the precious quarters exceedingly despoiled—
        the City of the Book,
            the abode of peace,
            builded with turrets.

Jerusalem is begirt with mountains,
Jerusalem is begirt with villages,
like nests of the vulture in the clefts of the rock—
but Jerusalem is a dove.

Has the smell of corpses risen to their nostrils,
that they have spread on every hand—
all-the-sons-of-Kedar in their multitudes?
A vulture upon thee, Jerusalem!
A viper upon thee, the beauty of all the lands!

The deer of Israel,
how have they plotted to hew down your horn!

ABRAHAM SHLONSKI

JERUSALEM today shows us the city divided against itself.
Barbed wire cuts off the old town, occupied by the Arabs, from
the new, capital of the State of Israel.

Gone is the calm of the days of peace
Whose face I have almost forgotten.
Here all is wide-open, howling silence, a dream.
The tendered bridge was only a mirage.
Over there I have seen gibbets and scaffolds . . .
This is the frontier and the blocking of roads.

Here the entrenched speak not the common tongue
they used in the market place and 'neath the porticoes.
Here wax mutual offenses
feeding their violence and their green manhood.
Standing, a man is target for gunsights;
Shelter must be sought in trenches alone.

From across no man speaks to his neighbour
nor seeks to woo him with the bread of friendship.
Over there, vengeance relies upon her stubborn one.
Old guardian of ancestral heritage.

How keep the innocent from his error?
One piles up those piles of stones
and nearby stand signposts, landmarks along the frontier,
and at their side, scarecrows flapping in the breeze.
And one must add, as peoples will,
deep lines well made with tears and blood.

H. GURI

What impressed me from the very first was the happiness and the pride of the children at play in the yard. We asked a number of them where they came from. Some came from Germany, others from Iraq, Turkey, and North Africa. Whatever their origin, in some way or another they had had to suffer for their birth. They belonged to a minority which, if not actively persecuted, was barely tolerated. Now they are in their own home among their own people and you can immediately feel that they are no longer oppressed by the burden of their race. They are like any other children with the good fortune to be growing up in their own country. Possibly their parents will always carry the scars of their upbringing, but not a trace can be found upon their children.

For their schooling, there is an obvious difference between their lessons and what is taught in our own classrooms. I cannot speak Hebrew, but it has become their mother tongue and their children find it no more difficult than our own children find French; but their national literature is the Old Testament . . .

JACQUES MADAULE

"Why did Abraham want to sacrifice Isaac? Why didn't he sacrifice himself? What harm had the poor little boy done?"

(Yehuda, aged five, the son of a school-master from Safed)

"Why does the Torah tell us to honour our parents and no book tell them to honour their children?"

(Miriam, aged seven, daughter of a civil servant from Tel Aviv)

The kindergarten mistress was telling the children about the Wailing Wall.

"Good," cried Jonathan, all smiles, "if they build the Temple now, they'll only have to put up three walls!"

(Jonathan, aged four and a half, Mochav, Kfar Hassidim)

SUBURB OF TEL AVIV

From the village yesterday
The warriors set out
Not to a war of fire and blood
But to harvest the golden grain.
Their weapons on their shoulders
No swords or guns—what then?
Hoes and scythes that sparkled
For to harvest the golden grain.

Oh they were very happy
To see the heavy ears.
The corn had grown so very high
It stood above their heads.
To the village in the evening
The warriors return
From no war of fire and blood
But from harvesting the grain.

(Oved, aged nine, from the farming village of Nahalal)

In the Class-room
Sit the children
Holding their pens
Clodhoppers no more.

They are writing poems
About the bright blue sky
About the silver moon
About the horse that gallops by.

One sings of donkeys
Another of—teachers
And big and small, all the children
Sing again in chorus
All happy, all glad: Hurrah!

Hurrah! We are poets!
Teachers will never call
The children of En Harod
Poor clodhoppers
For we are poets.

Joint poem written by the children of the kibbutz of
En Harod (ages between nine and ten) when a teacher
had called them "clodhoppers."

IN THE OLD TOWN, JAFFA

And if a stranger sojourn with thee in your land, ye shall not vex him. But the stranger that dwelleth with you shall be unto you as one born among you, and thou shalt love him as thyself...

LEVITICUS 19 : 33-34

Thou shalt neither vex a stranger, nor oppress him; for ye were strangers in the land of Egypt.

EXODUS 22 : 21

You will build your country so that the stranger will feel happy to be among you.

THEODOR HERZL. *The Jewish State.* 1895

Tel Aviv has grown from a garden suburb to be one of the most lively cities in the eastern Mediterranean. In 1909 there were five hundred and nine inhabitants, now the town is called Tel Aviv-Jaffa and has a population of about 350,000. Her builders called her Tel Aviv (Spring Hill) after a Babylonian town.

TEL AVIV: SAUSAGE VENDOR IN MOGRABI SQUARE

SUBURB OF TEL AVIV

TEL AVIV—CIGARETTE STAND ON ALLENBY ROAD

TEL AVIV—CONSTRUCTION WORKER

THE ILLS OF JOB

One day a Jew went to see his doctor.

"Oh, Doctor, I'm suffering dreadfully, I'm a second Job: I talk to myself."

Said the doctor:

"Really, that's nothing so dreadful: why even I do it myself sometimes. So what's all the fuss about?"

Answered the Jew:

"Of course, Doctor, but you don't understand. I'm such a terrible bore!"

NAPOLEON AND THE TAILOR

During the retreat from Moscow Napoleon chanced to be passing through a Jewish village when he saw a band of moujiks hot on his heels. The Emperor dashed into a little house in which a tailor lived and with a tremor in his voice said:

"Quickly, hide me, they are after my blood."

The tailor had no idea who the Emperor was. A man had asked him to save him, and save him he would.

So he told the Emperor:

"Just climb into bed, get under the eiderdown and don't move an inch whatever happens."

TEL AVIV: THE SEA FRONT

The Emperor lay down on the bed and the tailor covered him with first one eiderdown and then another and then a third and finally a fourth. He had hardly done so when the door burst open and in tumbled two moujiks waving their swords.

"Has anyone come in and hidden in your house?"

"No!" answered the Jew, "who would come in here and hide?"

The moujiks searched the house from top to bottom and even thrust their swords through the eiderdowns but there was nobody there. Then they left the way they had come. Once the door was shut behind them the Emperor slid out from under the eiderdowns, white as a sheet. Said he to the Jew:

"You must know that I am the Emperor Napoleon. You have saved me from certain death and in return you may ask me for any three things and whatever they are I shall give them to you."

The poor tailor thought a moment and then he said:

"Dear Emperor, would you mind mending the roof, you see this is the second year water has come through the ceiling."

"Booby! Idiot! Of course I'll have your roof repaired. Now ask me something good, and remember you have only two wishes left."

The poor tailor racked his brains: whatever could he ask? He thought and thought and at last he said:

"There's another tailor, here, in the same street, he takes all my customers, if only you would tell him to pack up and go."

"Dunderhead! Triple idiot! Of course I'll tell the other tailor to pack up and go—to the devil. Surely, though, you can ask for something more sensible than that. Now remember, one thing only."

When he heard this the tailor stood thinking, then with a smile he asked:

"I should like to know how you felt when the moujiks ran their swords through the eiderdowns."

The Emperor exploded.

"Impertinent jackanapes! How dare you ask me such a question. I'll have you shot for your insolence."

They took the Jew to prison. It is not hard to picture him shaking in his shoes especially when they told him he would be shot at dawn. The next day they led the tailor out and tied him to a tree. Three soldiers faced him, muskets to their shoulders while a fourth stood to one side and studied his watch. Soon he raised one arm and began to count: "One . . . two . . . thr . . ." But he never finished the word "three" for a general galloped up shouting "Halt! Don't shoot!" Then he said to the tailor:

"The Emperor pardons you and sends you this message."

The Jew heaved a great sigh and began to read the letter. All that was written was: "I felt just as you must have felt a moment ago!"

The tailor has carried the letter with him ever since.

Immigrant newly arrived from Rumania in a "maabarah" near Haifa.

PARABLES FROM THE HAGGADAH

It is written:

"Naked he came from his mother's womb, naked he shall return." (Eccl. 5:14)

Gueniba spoke this parable:

"A fox stood outside a vineyard that was fenced on every side. There was, however, one gap. The fox tried to slip through it but in vain for he was too fat. What did he do? He fasted three days and when he was thinner he got through the hole. Once within the vineyard he gave himself heart and soul to the feast and ate all the fruit he saw. But, he grew fat. To escape he must follow the same ritual, three days fast, then through the gap. Once outside he exclaimed: "Vineyard, vineyard, how good you are, how delicious your fruit! All within your fence is marvellous, but what use do you serve? I leave you in the same state as that in which I entered you!"

Such is the world.

When Noah began to plant his vineyard Satan appeared and asked him what he was doing.

"I am planting a vineyard," he explained.

"What is a vineyard?" asked Satan.

"Vines give fruit which is sweet both when it is fresh and when it is dried. From that fruit, too, is made wine which gladdens the heart."

"Would you like us to plant it together?"

"I would."

The bargain struck, Satan sacrificed, in order, a sheep, a lion, a monkey and a pig and sprinkled the vines with their blood.

Seeing Noah speechless Satan explained:

"After his first glass a man is as meek as a sheep; after his second he feels himself to be as brave as a lion, and becomes boastful; after his third and fourth, like the monkey he begins to dance, to play, and to talk foolishly, and when he is drunk he wallows in muck and filth like a hog."

RICHON LE-ZION. Bearing the proud name of "first in Zion," the colony was founded in 1882 and for many years was aided by Baron Edmond de Rothschild. Countless difficulties had to be surmounted, but now Richon Le-Zion is a centre of intensive cultivation. Her wines are exported abroad and her vintages have won a high reputation. It was here that the first Jewish kindergarten and the first primary school in the country were established.

O LEAD ME THOU, LORD

O lead me thou, Lord
And let me bear the measure of seed
On the ploughed fields of spring.
O let me bear the measure of seed
On my little parcel of land—
Till my last day is weaned
And stands before you
Like a tender stalk
That has bent its head full with grain:
"Cut me scythe for the time has come."

ABRAHAM SHLONSKI

Such a land, resettled by a new Jewish nation, tilled and watered by intelligent hands, warmed by the tropic sun, producing on its soil all the plants that men find necessary or delicious, from sugar cane and bananas to the vines and grains of the temperate regions and the cedars and pines of the Alps. Such a land, I repeat, would be the Promised Land of our day if Providence were to give it a people, and the tide of world affairs peace and freedom.

LAMARTINE
(1790–1869)

THE VALLEY OF HOULI: MT. HERMON

In the first place the houses of the Essenes are not privately owned by one but, when need arises, are common to all, for over and above that they live in communities of brothers their houses are open to all of the same sect who come from elsewhere. And then there is one purse to supply the needs of all and they share all expenses, while clothing and food is shared in the same way, and, in fact, they take their meals together. For nowhere else can be found the practice of the same lodging for all, the same way of life for all, the same food for all, better put into effect. And not without reason, for all the money they receive for their day's work is put to the common benefit of all who wish to profit thereby.

PHILO of Alexandria
(20 B.C.–47 A.D.?)

K'vusah Dagania, oldest of the Hebrew Communes, stood in the Jordan Valley at the southern tip of the Lake of Tiberias. It had been founded in 1911 by ten boys and two girls from Romni in Poland, who had decided to put theory into practice and embarked on the first experiment in rural communism. They shared everything—earnings, food, clothes, the Arab mud huts which were their first living quarters, the mosquitoes and bugs, the night-watches against Bedouins and robbers, malaria, typhoid and sand-fly fever; everything except their beds, for, true to romantic tradition, they lived for a number of years in self-imposed chastity. They refused to employ hired labour, to handle money except in their dealings with the outside world, and even to mark their shirts before they went to the communal laundry for fear that the bug of individual possessiveness might start breeding in them. They regarded themselves as the spiritual heirs of the Essenes who, fleeing from the shallow glamour of Jerusalem, had founded in the desert their communities based on the sharing of labour and its fruits. They had studied the Bible, Marx and Herzl, and knew neither how to plant a tree nor how to milk a cow. The Arabs thought they were madmen and the old Jewish planters in Judaea thought the Commune of the Twelve a bad joke and a heresy. Yet today Dagania's third generation was being brought up in the communal nurseries on the same mad Essene principles, while more than a hundred other Hebrew communal villages had spread all over the country, from the Mediterranean to the Dead Sea and from Dan to Beersheba. . . . All of them had the same basic features: the communal dining-hall, workshops and children's house; the prohibition of hired labour; the abolition of money, barter and private property; the sharing of the work according to everyone's capacity and of its produce according to his needs.

ARTHUR KOESTLER
(Thieves in the Night)

134

KING SOLOMON'S MINES: THE CANTEEN. These miners, who work in the ancient copper mines of King Solomon, came from different countries and are of differing backgrounds: student, electrician and wireless mechanic. The girl was born in Paris and worked as a typist, now she shares the life of these miners in the heart of the Negev, a desert where the temperature tops 104 degrees in the shade. As an immigrant she did her two years military service (compulsory for all girls) in the Negev and stayed on. As camp hostess she cheers the lives of the three hundred or so miners who have left all to revive these ancient mines.

The peasants of Israel were out in the field—the ripe wheat fields—of Bethlehem. They swung their sickles among the ears of wheat and sang "Those that sow in tears shall reap in joy." Some were binding sheaves, on their lips the song: "He that goeth forth and weepeth, bearing precious seed, shall doubtless come again with rejoicing, bringing his sheaves with him." Others were carrying sheaves to the barns as they sang: "My wheat knelt and bowed down to my sheaf. Lord give me strength that I may fill my barns."

And the fields rang out with the sound of work and songs.

In this season, also Eliav, accompanied by his wife and two sons, set out for his patch of land to start reaping. And Eliav, his wife and two sons, entered from the four corners into the field where the wheat abounded. They were all submerged, for the tall and heavy ears of wheat covered them completely, and one could not tell there were people in the wheat field. But before long their sickles started swaying back and forth flashing in the peasants' skilful hands, and as the ears of wheat fell on all sides, the heads of the reapers soon rose above the golden sea.

Catching sight of him, a neighbour cried out to Eliav:

"From your wheat field to your barn, neighbour!"

And Eliav, returning blessing for blessing:

"From your vineyard to your wine-cellar, my good neighbour!"

"The Lord's blessing upon you, neighbour!" cried out Eliav's wife (to their neighbour's wife). "Have you already washed the wool of your sheep?"

"The Lord be with you, my neighbour," she answered; "washed and even carded!"

"And I have already woven some of my yarn!"

"May the Lord bless us and give us strength for many years to come!"

Eliav's sickle whirred among the ears of wheat and seemed to say, "Be silent, women! It is time to return to work!"

The women cut short their conversation and the sickles swung again among the ears of wheat.

And one could hear only the whirring of sickles in the wheat fields.

JUDAH STEINBERG

The festival of Omer. The harvest festival is being celebrated in the farming colony of Kvutzat Schiller. In this way the Israeli labourers renew a link with an extremely ancient Hebrew custom. In days gone by the peasants of Israel would go out into their fields on the evening of the first day of the Passover, and, amid general festivity, cut the first ripe ears of wheat.

An only kid, an only kid
my father bought
for two zuzím.
An only kid, an only kid.

And came a cat
that ate the kid
My father bought
for two zuzím.

Song from the Haggadah

THE KID FROM THE HAGGADAH

Among he-goats and she-goats, in the market it stood
and wiggled its tail
that was small as your pinky.
A kid bred by poor folks, his price two zuzím,
unadorned,
without ribbon or trinket.

No one noticed it there, for none of them knew,
not the wool-carders, goldsmiths, none of that throng,
that this very kid into legend would go,
be the hero of a song.

But my father approached with radiant face,
and bought that kid,
its muzzle caressing . . .
The beginning this was of one of those tales
shall be sung for aye, with a blessing.

A spring day it was, and the breezes danced,
and the winking girls laughed, as bright as the weather.
And Father and the Kid
into Legend stepped,
and stood in the Haggadah, together.

NATHAN ALTERMAN

KIBBUTZ DAPHNE

THE SIGNS OF THE ZODIAC (Fifth-century mosaic from the Synagogue of Beth-Alpha).

THE UPLANDS OF CARMEL

THE SONG OF SOLOMON

7. *Tell me, O thou whom my soul loveth, where thou feedest, where thou makest thy flock to rest at noon: for why should I be as one that turneth aside by the flocks of thy companions?*

8. *If thou know not, O thou fairest among women, go thy way forth by the footsteps of the flock, and feed thy kids beside the shepherds' tents.*

Chapter 1

7. *I charge you, O ye daughters of Jerusalem, by the roes, and by the hinds of the field, that ye stir not up, nor awake my love, till he please.*

8. *The voice of my beloved! behold, he cometh leaping upon the mountains, skipping upon the hills.*

9. *My beloved is like a roe or a young hart: behold, he standeth behind our wall, he looketh forth at the windows, shewing himself through the lattice.*

10. *My beloved spake, and said unto me, Rise up, my love, my fair one, and come away.*

11. *For, lo, the winter is past, the rain is over and gone;*

12. *The flowers appear on the earth; the time of the singing is come, and the voice of the turtle is heard in our land;*

13. *The fig tree putteth forth her green figs, and the vines with the tender grape give a good smell. Arise, my love, my fair one, and come away.*

Chapter 2

9. *Thou hast ravished my heart, my sister, my spouse; thou hast ravished my heart with one of thine eyes, with one chain of thy neck.*

10. *How fair is thy love, my sister, my spouse! how much better is thy love than wine! and the smell of thine ointments than all spices!*

11. *Thy lips, O my spouse, drop as the honeycomb: honey and milk are under thy tongue; and the smell of thy garments is like the smell of Lebanon.*

12. *A garden enclosed is my sister, my spouse; a spring shut up, a fountain sealed.*

Chapter 4

6. *I opened to my beloved; but my beloved had withdrawn himself, and was gone: my soul failed when he spake: I sought him, but I could not find him; I called him, but he gave me no answer.*

7. *The watchmen that went about the city found me, they smote me, they wounded me; the keepers of the walls took away my veil from me.*

THE VALLEY OF SHARON

8. *I charge you, O daughters of Jerusalem, if ye find my beloved, that ye tell him, that I am sick of love.*

Chapter 5

1. *How beautiful are thy feet with shoes, O prince's daughter! the joints of thy thighs are like jewels, the work of the hands of a cunning workman.*
2. *Thy navel is like a round goblet, which wanteth not liquor: thy belly is like an heap of wheat set about with lilies.*
3. *Thy two breasts are like two young roes that are twins.*
4. *Thy neck is as a tower of ivory; thine eyes like the fishpools in Heshbon, by the gate of Bathrabbim: thy nose is as the tower of Lebanon which looketh toward Damascus.*
5. *Thine head upon thee is like Carmel, and the hair of thine head like purple; the king is held in the galleries.*
6. *How fair and how pleasant are thou, O love, for delights!*
10. *I am my beloved's, and his desire is toward me.*
11. *Come, my beloved, let us go forth into the field; let us lodge in the villages.*
12. *Let us get up early to the vineyards; let us see if the vine flourish, whether the tender grape appear, and the pomegranates bud forth: there will I give thee my loves.*

Chapter 7

1. *O that thou wert as my brother, that sucked the breasts of my mother! when I should find thee without, I would kiss thee; yea, I should not be despised.*
2. *I would lead thee, and bring thee into my mother's house, who would instruct me: I would cause thee to drink of spiced wine of the juice of my pomegranate.*
3. *His left hand should be under my head, and his right hand should embrace me.*
4. *I charge you, O daughters of Jerusalem, that ye stir not up, nor awake my love until he please.*
6. *Set me as a seal upon thine heart, as a seal upon thine arm: for love is strong as death; jealousy is cruel as the grave: the coals thereof are coals of fire, which hath a most vehement flame.*
7. *Many waters cannot quench love, neither can the floods drown it: if a man would give all the substance of his house for love, it would utterly be contemned.*

Chapter 8

DETAIL OF A THIRD-CENTURY FRESCO IN THE SYNAGOGUE OF DOURA-EUROPOS

BEERSHEBA. Capital of the Negev, it owes its name (Seven Wells) to Abraham who sunk seven wells there. (Genesis 22.) It is one of the most ancient places in the region. An outpost of the Bedouin, Beersheba is in the throes of becoming the great town of the desert and already possesses the largest cinema in the country.

MASSADAH. On the western shore of the Dead Sea facing the peninsular, the cliffs drop sheer down to the rock. On one of these cliffs the ancient and inaccessible Jewish fortress of Massadah was set. After Titus had captured Jerusalem and destroyed the Temple (70 A.D.) his legions besieged Massadah where the Jewish troops offered a stubborn resistance for three years. Traces of the Jewish fortress and the besiegers lines still exist. Young Israelis often make the pilgrimage to Massadah which is to them the symbol of the resistance.

This is how the contemporary historian Flavius Josephus describes the resistance of the Jews to the Roman invader:

The Roman general led his army against Massadah, occupied by Eleazar and the terrorists. He quickly seized the surrounding country and posted troops on all commanding positions. He then raised a wall around it to make it difficult for the besieged to escape, and he set sentries on it.

Eleazar, however, had no thought of flight, nor did he allow anyone to flee ... He could envisage no means of escape or defence, and when he thought of the treatment that the

Girl on the road to Massadah. Her name is Sulamite, Bat-Sheba or Miriam. She is doing her military service with Nahal (Young Pioneers' Army). This lasts two years of which one year is spent in farming or in general pioneering work.

Romans, once masters of the place, would inflict upon the defenders, their wives and their children, he determined that they all must die.

Having taken this decision, the best under the circumstances, he assembled the bravest of his comrades and exhorted them to act thus, in this speech.

"Long ago we resolved never to serve the Romans or any person other than the one true God, the only just master of mankind; the hour has now come which commands us to confirm our resolve by deeds. Now that it has come let us not shame ourselves, we who have hitherto scorned slavery and safety, and who are now exposed to inexorable punishment as well as slavery if the Romans take us alive, for we were the first to rebel and we are the last to remain in arms against them. I think, moreover, that we have received God's especial favour in that we are enabled to die nobly as free men, whereas others, conquered against all expectation, have not had this privilege. Tomorrow the capture of this place stares us in the face, but so too does the freedom to choose a noble death and share it with our dearest friends. For the enemy who so ardently desires to take us alive can do as little to prevent our resolve as we can to snatch victory from them in battle.
"Death then for our wives, not rape; death for our children, not slavery! When we have killed them let us render the same generous service the one to the other, and let freedom be our noble shroud. But first let us burn the treasures in our fortress, for I know well that the Romans will grieve to forfeit their mastership of our persons and to be deprived of their plunder. Let us leave only our provisions to bear us witness when we are dead that, unvanquished by hunger, we were faithful to our first resolve and preferred death to slavery."

He would have continued to exhort them but filled with an irresistible enthusiasm they hastened to accomplish what he had advised.

FLAVIUS JOSEPHUS
(37–100 A.D.)

KING SOLOMON'S PILLARS. The Old Testament tells how, in the time of Moses, bronze was made in Edom, near the Red Sea. The Chronicles place the copper mines of King Solomon in the same region. "Now Solomon departed unto Etzion-Gever and Eloth on the shores of the sea in the land of Edom" (II Chron. 8:17). Recently experts have discovered copper scoria in this region. An ambitious scheme has been put in hand to exploit these mines and countless shafts have been sunk.

And I will make all my mountains a way, and my highways shall be exalted.

Behold, these shall come from far; and, lo, these from the north and from the west; and these from the land of Sinim.

Sing, O Heavens; and be joyful, O earth; and break forth into singing, O mountains ...

ISAIAH 49:11-13

THE HILLS OF JERUSALEM

Watchman, what of the night?
Watchman, what of the night?
The watchman said,
The morning cometh, and also the night.

ISAIAH 21:11-12